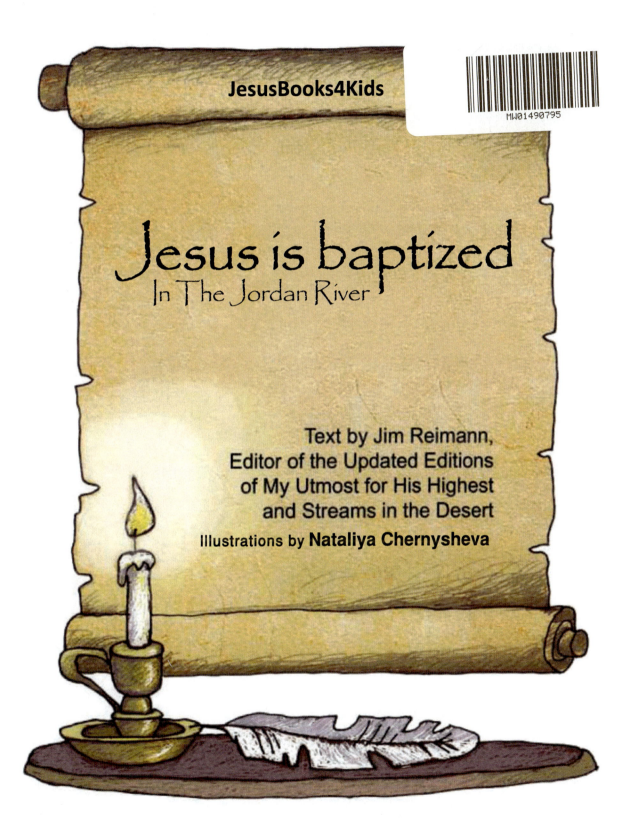

JesusBooks4Kids

MW01490795

Jesus is baptized
In The Jordan River

Text by Jim Reimann,
Editor of the Updated Editions
of My Utmost for His Highest
and Streams in the Desert

Illustrations by **Nataliya Chernysheva**

In the Holy Land, just east of Jericho
By the Jordan River, is a quiet, peaceful place.
Qasr al-Yahud, the Castle of the Jews, you know.
It's where thousands come every year,
                                    by God's grace.

4

6

It is at Qasr al-Yahud that people step into the river—
Dozens of white-robed believers every single day.
Often the water is cool, so the people may begin to shiver;
Still they come—to follow Christ in baptism and pray.

Pilgrim after pilgrim, from nation after nation,
Confessing and repenting of their sins and their wrongs,
Some in their ethnic garb travel to this location
To renew their faith, and sing sacred songs.

It was to this very Jordan—the ancient Yarden,
Which Joshua once crossed, with Israelites so many,
That John the Baptist came to baptize—way back when,
For the river had much water—water aplenty.

11

John was unlike the religious leaders of his day,
For he wore a leather belt and clothes of camel's hair.
Along with speaking truth they didn't expect he'd say,
He ate locusts and honey, and was a man of prayer.

There, by the gently flowing, winding Jordan River,
John preached, "Repent, for the kingdom of heaven is near."
He shared the words God had given him to deliver—
A desert voice calling out to those who would hear.

Many came, confessed their sins, and were baptized by John;
"I baptize with water for repentance," he told them all,
"But when the Messiah of God arrives," John went on,
"He will baptize with the Spirit, as you hear His call."

John was not the Messiah, as we know from God's Word,
For Isaiah foretold John would prepare Jesus' way.
And one day it happened by Yarden—John saw the Lord.
Jesus the Christ walked straight toward him—this must be the day!

Yet John, a man whose heart was quite humble and contrite,
Felt unworthy to remove the sandals of the Lord.
But Jesus, said, "Let it be so now, for this is right;
To fulfill what is said in My Father's Holy Word."

17

So John baptized the Lord, but before he was all done,
God's heavenly Spirit fell on Jesus as a dove.
His Father then lovingly said, "You are my dear Son;
With you I am very pleased, and the One whom I love."

It was then that Jesus began to preach the good news,
For the Lord's ministry began on that very day.
Speaking to all the boys and girls, Gentiles and Jews,
He said to be saved from sin, He alone was THE WAY.

Now there is a place on the Jordan River called Qasr al Yahud
Where pilgrims flock for a holy baptism in waters filled with good.
With joy in their hearts, their prayers and song fill the air
They make a promise to God and all feel His love everywhere.

Qasr al Yahud Baptism Site - The Traditional Site of Jesus' Baptism

Over a half-million Christians come each year from all over the world
to Qasr al Yahud, the actual site of the Baptism of Jesus.
They get baptized in the waters of the Jordan River, some for the first time
in their lives and others to make a rededication of their life to the Lord.
The experience of the immersion in the living waters at the Qasr al Yahud site
is very much like the Biblical immersion in the days of Jesus and his disciples.
The baptismal pool is shaped like a cross and the flowing waters
of the Jordan Rivers constantly fill it naturally and cleanly.
Visitors seeking to be baptized take ancient marble steps into the Jordan River
which makes for a special and unique baptismal experience.
The age of these steps is not known, but they were mentioned the first time
1400 years ago. Many of the innumerable pilgrims visiting Qasr al Yahud
through the ages have carved little crosses into the stone, which can still
be seen, giving the site a feeling of history and unity with Christians
from all places and times.
For the convenience of visitors, the site has a wooden deck for viewing Baptisms.

Qasr al Yahud is located on the road to Jericho from Jerusalem and numerous churches were built here over the centuries. The site is also significant in the Jewish tradition, as it is believed to be the place where the Children of Israel crossed the Jordan when they entered Canaan.
The area is amazingly beautiful, and the trail to the Jordan is very tranquil, like an oasis. The visitors' facilities have been given the utmost care, with clear access to the river, showers and facilities for prayer. It is also wheelchair-accessible.

The site is under the administration of the Israel Parks Authority. Visitors may purchase meaningful souvenirs, such as small bottles of Jordan River water, to take home.

23

for ordering:

Intelecty Ltd. Publishing House

76 Hagalil St.

Nofit 36001

Israel

Tel: +97249930922

Fax: +972722830147

amirarkind@gmail.com

Printed in the Holy Land

FOR INFORMATION

TEL: STORE: 97226504844

TEL: OFFICE: 97226726188

JesusBooks4Kids

Printed by GESTELIT
info@gestelit.co.il

More in the series:

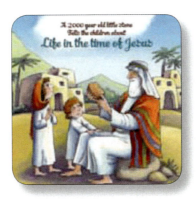

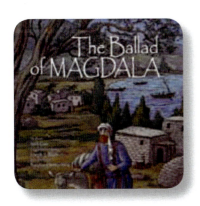

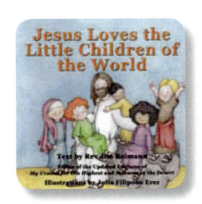

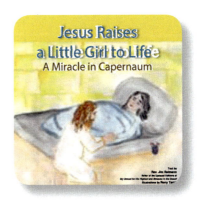

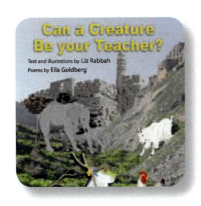

Made in the USA
Monee, IL
28 May 2025

18305048R00017